JOHN GREEN

ALL ABOUT THE AUTHOR™

JOHN GREEN

CHRISTINE POOLOS

ROSEN
PUBLISHING®

New York

Published in 2015 by The Rosen Publishing Group, Inc.
29 East 21st Street, New York, NY 10010

Library of Congress Cataloging-in-Publication Data

Poolos, Christine.
John Green/Christine Poolos.—First edition.
        pages cm.—(All about the author)
Includes bibliographical references and index.
ISBN 978-1-4777-7904-0 (library bound)
1. Green, John, 1977—Juvenile literature. 2. Authors, American--21st century—Biography—Juvenile literature. I. Title.
PS3607.R432928Z84 2015
813'.6—dc23
[B]

2014007271

Manufactured in China

CONTENTS

On January 15, 2013, more than 2,800 concertgoers streamed into New York City's Carnegie Hall. Throughout its history, the world-famous venue had hosted such musical luminaries as George Gershwin, Leonard Bernstein, Maria Callas, and the Beatles. So who was the musician that this crowd was so excited to see on such a cold evening?

The man who had sold out Carnegie Hall just ten days after announcing the event was John Green. Green is not a musician at all but a writer of young adult novels. He was taking the stage, along with his brother, Hank Green, for an event they called "An Evening of Awesome," a variety show celebrating the one-year anniversary of John's latest novel, *The Fault in Our Stars*. The concertgoers packed into Carnegie Hall were mostly teenagers, but there were plenty of adults as well. Many wore "Nerdfighter," "DFTBA," or "Pizza John" T-shirts. Some carried copies of Green's books.

At a time when publishers are concerned that people have stopped reading and book sales have dropped, how is it that a writer can sell nearly three thousand tickets to a live variety show?

John Green is a best-selling author, video blogger, and advocate. He has been named one of *Time* magazine's one hundred most influential people in the world.

John Green first grabbed the attention of young adults and school librarians with the publication of his first novel, *Looking for Alaska*, in 2005. In the coming years he would write four more at the rate of about one every two years.

With each book he gained more critical awards and loyal readers. But it may be his side job as a YouTube star that boosted his fan base the most. As video-blog duo the Vlogbrothers, John and Hank Green spew facts at rapid rates, talk about their humiliating teenage moments, exact punishments on one another for various infractions, and do just about anything else you can imagine. They also raise money for charitable causes as part of their Project for Awesome.

Their viewership is so strong that YouTube recruited them for an educational venture they call CrashCourse featuring short, entertaining mini-courses on history and science.

Green's ability to engage with his audience through social media like YouTube, Twitter, and Tumblr resulted in the formation of an extended community that has taken on a life of its own. They call themselves "nerdfighters," and they fight for intellectualism. They are not ashamed to be smart and to enjoy Harry Potter a little too much. And they are working to do good in the world.

Nerdfighters screamed and cheered in esteemed Carnegie Hall as John and Hank Green took the stage dressed, improbably, in tuxes. Hank sang some of his novelty tunes. John's favorite band, the Mountain Goats, performed. Guest stars, including powerhouse author Neil Gaiman, assisted in readings and a Q&A session that promised that one of the brothers would get an electric shock by the end.

In the most moving portion of the evening, John Green spoke about the power of books, especially the power that *The Fault in Our Stars* had for him and now has for its readers. He talked about the nerdfighter Esther Earl, whose loss to cancer compelled Green to write the story he'd been trying to write for a decade.

But for the most part he was entertaining, funny, intelligent, enthusiastic, and just plain giddy to be performing in Carnegie Hall in front of nearly three thousand people who had paid to see him. He was exactly what nerdfighters expected.

THE GREAT PERHAPS

While John Green's fans often look for clues to his life in his novels, they would be wise to show restraint in making assumptions about the author. It may be true that some events in his novels are based on real-life happenings and that some of his characters share elements with himself. However, it is important to note that John Green is a talented writer with a creative imagination and not everything he writes can be traced back to his own life.

A PORTRAIT OF THE ARTIST AS A YOUNG MAN

John Michael Green was born on August 24, 1977, in Indianapolis, Indiana. When he was still an infant, his family moved to Orlando, Florida. Nearly three years later, John's

Growing up, Green was bullied and had difficulty making friends. These experiences drove him to seek refuge in books.

brother, Hank, was born. The boys grew up in a happy family, thanks to their parents, Mike (a nature conservancy director) and Sydney (a community organizer). On his website, Green notes that he was "extremely fortunate [because] my parents loved and encouraged me [and] my brother was empathetic and supportive."

Growing up in Florida was a mixed bag for Green. He described the state to the *Seattle Post Intelligencer* as "a mix of transience and insularity inherent to most of suburban life." He would use this notion of transience to great effect in his novel *Paper Towns.*

Green admits that he had some challenges while growing up. He suffered from anxiety and insecurity. This made it difficult for him to make friends. A self-described nerd and a voracious reader (especially J. D. Salinger's and Toni Morrison's books), he was anything but popular, although he did have a few close friends. Looking back, Green states on his website, "I think I was quite difficult to be around. ... I was really super-self-absorbed."

He also says he was bullied in school, and perhaps these factors contributed to his desire to get away. John moved away from home to board at the private Indian Springs School in Alabama. This experience changed his life profoundly. At Indian Springs, it was not unusual to be smart and to want to know things. In a way, it was cool to be a nerd. John made friends,

LIFE AS A CLASSROOM

Many years after graduating, John Green found himself in a teaching position. In the first installment of his CrashCourse Internet series, he interrupts his own introduction to ask, in the voice of a student, "Mr. Green, Mr. Green! Is this gonna be on the test?" Green's brilliant answer is the best advice a student could get:

> Yeah, about the test: The test will measure whether you are an informed, engaged, and productive citizen of the world, and it will take place in schools and bars and hospitals and dorm rooms and in places of worship. You will be tested on first dates, in job interviews, while watching football, and while scrolling through your Twitter feed.
>
> The test will judge your ability to think about things other than celebrity marriages; whether you'll be easily persuaded by empty political rhetoric; and whether you'll be able to place your life and your community in a broader context.
>
> The test will last your entire life, and it will be comprised of the millions of decisions that, when taken together, make your life yours. And everything—everything—will be on it. I know, right? So pay attention.

met girls, was heavily influenced by teachers, and came out of his shell. "Attending Indian Springs made my life possible," Green says on his website, "and I am very grateful to the school and its teachers."

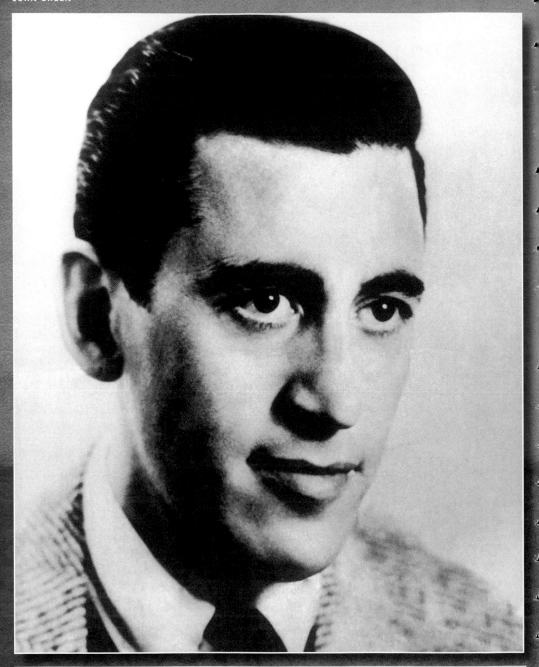

One of Green's favorite authors is J. D. Salinger. Salinger's characters are often highly intelligent and feel alienated from society.

Indian Wells serves as the inspiration for the setting of Green's first book, *Looking for Alaska*. In that novel, Miles, the protagonist, leaves a friendless existence in Florida for a boarding school called Culver Creek. While there, he forms close friendships, falls in love, drinks, smokes, plays pranks, and experiences profound loss. Green takes great pains to inform readers that *Looking for Alaska* is not his life story. However, he admits that of all his books, it is the most autobiographical. Given this statement, it is hard not to conclude after reading the book that Indian Springs was where John Green came of age, much like his own Miles, and like Holden Caulfield, the hero of J. D. Salinger's *The Catcher in the Rye*.

FINDING HIMSELF AT KENYON

After graduating from Indian Springs, Green attended Kenyon College in Gambier, Ohio. If Indian Springs was an opportunity for young John Green to find like-minded people and form deep friendships, Kenyon was the place that allowed him to grow and find himself.

In a video blog, Green says, "I was an undistinguished student, but I was smart enough to surround myself with very smart people." At Kenyon, Green expanded his realm of literature. Two important works that he read during this time were Zadie Smith's debut novel, *White Teeth*, and David Foster

Wallace's masterpiece, *Infinite Jest.* Putting his love of reading to work, he majored in English.

He also majored in religious studies. Raised as an Episcopalian, Green had grown up surrounded by faith. But his interest in studying religion at Kenyon came from an academic place. "It was 1999, and I was interested in interreligious dialogue between Christians and Muslims," he told Goodreads.com.

These two majors might seem disparate to some, but Green found strong ties between them, using the texts to understand himself and the world. Green described to Goodreads the experience of reading the roughly 1,100-page novel *Infinite Jest* twice during his freshman year at Kenyon:

> It was hugely important to me, and there were times when I felt like I was almost reading scripture, prophecy, not just great fiction but something tremendously relevant to my life on a minute-by-minute basis. It's still deeply relevant, not just to how I think about fiction but how I approach the world every morning.
>
> [Wallace's] idea that the central obligation of the human being is to be observant, to respond to what to you see empathically and compassionately, which is at the center of all of his work really, that idea is a guiding principle in my life.

Green had a rigorous academic course load but made time for pleasure reading. Somehow, he found time to read the hulking *Infinite Jest* twice during his first year.

Green also took creative writing classes in college. It is natural to assume that, in studying English and pursuing creative writing, Green had planned on becoming a writer. It turns out that this was all great preparation for being a best-selling author, but Green didn't know it at the time. "I knew I loved books from a very early age and always dreamt of writing them," he wrote to a fan in a live chat for *People* magazine. "But I never thought I would be an author professionally. It seemed like being an astronaut or something."

KENYON'S INFLUENCE

At Kenyon, Green challenged himself with a four-student class that focused solely on James Joyce's notoriously

Attending Kenyon College was a life-changing experience for Green. Even though he left its halls years ago, he is active in student recruitment efforts.

difficult novel *Ulysses*. This rigorous class "was the first time I ever felt academically grown up," he says. Green also made important, lasting friendships, cemented by bonding experiences such as cross-country road trips and a summer job in Alaska. One friend from the *Ulysses* class was Ransom Riggs, future author of the popular young adult novel *Miss Peregrine's Home for Peculiar Children.* The friends later shared the two top spots on the *New York Times* best-seller list.

The school also served as inspiration for the novels Green would later write. The campus's Church of the Holy Spirit is a cruciform construction, just like the church that houses Hazel's support group in *The Fault in Our Stars.* Green modeled the Old Man in *Looking for Alaska* after Kenyon religion professor Don Rogan.

Kenyon meant so much to John Green that he has offered his services in the college's efforts to recruit new students. In a series of highly entertaining short video promotions for the school called "Pensive Moments with John Green," Green ruminates on various subjects of interest to perspective students, ranging from academics to sports to food to famous alumni.

"One of the most terrifying aspects of selecting a college," he says in one short, looking into the

camera, "is the inner monologue of 'Will I fit in?'
Well—SPOILER ALERT!—you're going to change
in about a million ways, so a better question is,
'Will this college allow me to grow?'" The admissions department's tactic of using a beloved YA
author to draw the country's best students seems
to be working. According to the Kenyon *Collegian*,
"Of Kenyon's roughly 4,000 applicants last year,
275 hopeful students referenced Green in their
applications."

Green seems to have gained as much as he
could from his college experience, and indeed he
is more than grateful to his beloved institution. He
graduated from Kenyon with a degree, good friends,
and a passion for life.

STRUGGLES PAY OFF

Leaving the comfortable bubble of college, with nurturing professors and friends who are always available to take the next adventure with you, for the so-called real world can lead to intense culture shock. Green had a plan in mind for his future, but he could never have guessed the turns his life would take.

STUDENT CHAPLAIN

After graduation, Green enrolled at the University of Chicago Divinity School. His plan was to become an Episcopal priest. Green was interested in continuing to ask the big questions that theological studies explore.

Part of the process of becoming ordained as a minister is called discernment, making sure

After graduating from Kenyon, Green enrolled at the University of Chicago's Divinity School. He intended to devote his life to exploring deep theological issues.

a person understands what is involved in pursuing the ministry. An early step in the discernment process is called clinical pastoral education. This means a candidate must gain practical experience working as a chaplain. Chaplains are religious leaders who work in secular institutions, such as schools, military units, prisons, and police or fire departments.

Green wanted to do his clinical pastoral education at a children's hospital. In a hospital setting, a chaplain helps patients, family, and staff cope with the myriad emotional needs that accompany illness, dying, and death.

Green worked at a children's hospital in Ohio for five months. In all, the experience was as valuable and important as he had imagined it would be. But it also was more deeply crushing than he expected. In a story he later wrote for the National Public Radio (NPR) program "All Things Considered," Green remembers a father he calls "Nick," who brought his toddler in to the emergency room. Green could tell she would not survive. As he prayed with Nick, it became clear to Green that the injury had not been an accident, as the man had claimed. Indeed, after his daughter's death Nick eventually confessed to the authorities that he was responsible for harming the girl.

This incident shook Green's beliefs and his plans for the future:

> I abandoned my dream of ordained ministry shortly after reading about Nick's confession in the newspaper. I hated Nick, and while good chaplains can faint, maybe, they cannot hate. ...
>
> Until I met Nick, I always had faith in the possibility of redemption, but no one could save Nick, and I didn't want him to be redeemed. I wanted, and want, Nick to suffer. If I could wish him peace, I could probably be a good chaplain.

After five months of this intense work, Green had serious doubts. "I found myself really unfulfilled by the answers that are traditionally offered to questions of why some people suffer and why others suffer so little," he told the *Sydney Morning Herald*. Suddenly, he was unsure about his plans. Did he really want to lead his own church?

Not only was he supposed to attend divinity school, but he also had committed to sharing an apartment in Chicago with friends. Others were counting on him. This feeling of pressure and uncertainty began a period of depression and self-doubt for Green. It would be years before he was able to see how useful his chaplain experience was to him as a person, and as a writer.

A TURNING POINT

Green left Ohio and moved to Chicago as he had promised, but he deferred admission to divinity school. He signed on with a temp agency, which eventually placed him with *Booklist*, a journal published by the American Library Association. *Booklist* reviews thousands of new books every year and recommends those that librarians should add to their collections.

Like many recent college graduates, Green found his job monotonous and intellectually unfulfilling. Rather than reading and writing, he was entering ten-digit codes into a computer all day. He had the good fortune, however, of working with a wonderful group of people who taught him much about writing and editing, and about life in general.

In addition, as thousands of published books rolled into the offices, Green began to realize that thousands of authors had written those books. And that meant that maybe the profession of writing wasn't as unattainable as he had once thought.

LEAVE OF ABSENCE

By the age of twenty-four, Green was happy at his job at *Booklist*, living in an apartment in a city he loved with his girlfriend and their cat. Then he and his girlfriend broke up, and Green went into a depression. (Green has said that in retrospect, the breakup didn't cause his depression but was more likely due to it.)

Suddenly Green felt hopeless. He'd been trying to write a novel, but he wasn't having success with it. His girlfriend was gone. Although he'd deferred admission to divinity school, he continued to believe in the possibility of returning at some point, but he didn't think that was what he wanted. Nothing seemed to be right in his life. He even lost interest in eating.

He knew enough to call his parents for help, and they insisted he return to Orlando. Green intended to quit his job at *Booklist* in order to concentrate on healing, but his kindly publisher suggested taking a two-week leave of absence instead.

In Orlando, Green attended daily therapy sessions. His doctors adjusted his medication. And, perhaps both as part of the healing process and a result of it, he began writing in earnest. At the end of two weeks, he returned to Chicago with a changed perspective on his life.

HARVEY

When Green took a leave of absence from *Booklist*, his concerned publisher suggested he watch the classic movie *Harvey*. This 1950 film stars Jimmy Stewart as Elwood P. Dowd, a middle-aged man whose best friend is Harvey, a 6-foot (1.8-meter) tall invisible rabbit.

It is unclear to Elwood's family (and to the viewer) whether Harvey is a manifestation of Elwood's

Green credits the movie *Harvey* with helping him gain perspective on life while being treated for depression.

fondness for drink or perhaps a mental illness. But eventually, they all become convinced of the existence of Elwood's companion.

Thinking back to this time, in a video blog Green says that, along with therapy and medication, after watching *Harvey*, he stopped feeling quite so bad: "One line really did change my life: Elwood says, 'My mother used to tell me that in this world, Elwood, you must be oh so smart or oh so pleasant. Well, for years I was smart. I recommend pleasant.'"

CONNECTING WITH A MENTOR

Green's life didn't suddenly turn into a fairy tale, but his outlook did improve. Eventually, he was given more responsibility at *Booklist*. He began to write reviews for the many books that poured in to the offices, including literary fiction.

One day at the *Booklist* offices, Green approached his colleague, editor and writer Ilene Cooper. He told her about a piece he'd been writing. Cooper agreed to serve as a mentor to Green, whom she found bright and engaging.

Six months later, in early 2002, Green brought Cooper a story he'd written about a tragedy at a boarding school. Over the next two years, Cooper helped him develop the work until it was ready to send out to publishers. This manuscript would become *Looking for Alaska.*

Green credits much of his success to Cooper's talent as an editor, mentor, champion, and friend. The two are still friends and mutual advisers. Paying it forward, Green tries to do for other young writers what Cooper so generously did for him.

PUBLIC RADIO

Although Green still had his day job, his writing output increased. With his friend, comedian and writer Claire Zulkey, he started a reading series for humor writing called "Funny Ha-Ha." A connection to writer Amy Krouse Rosenthal in 2002 led to appearances on "Writer's Block Party," a program she hosted on Chicago's public radio station. Green was a natural performer on air. His pieces were well received.

The transcripts of his public radio essays are posted on Green's website. They are short, funny bits, mostly about starting out and living in Chicago. Reading them, you can see Green finding his voice, letting his humor shine, and learning the simple act of how to tell a story that people want to listen to.

Green continued to contribute to Chicago Public Radio and, occasionally, NPR's prestigious program "All Things Considered," for several years.

Mentors like Ilene Cooper, and editors Julie Strauss-Gabel and Saskia Heinz *(above, with Green)*, help Green through the difficult process of writing and promoting books. Green believes the books are just as much theirs as his.

THINGS REALLY BEGIN TO LOOK UP

John Green famously—perhaps even proudly—remarks that he has been dumped fifty-three times. The factoid is even in his author biography for *An Abundance of Katherines.* Gregarious, funny, and nice-looking, Green certainly didn't have trouble attracting girlfriends. He did, however, have trouble keeping them.

This pattern seemed doomed to continue when he met Sarah Urist, a beautiful and vibrant young art gallery assistant, at a house party. In a remarkable coincidence, Urist had attended Indian Springs during the time Green was there, although the two were not friends. Green was instantly smitten but experienced the same nerves as many of his characters when it came to asking her out.

You might say their first date was based on a lie. Green e-mailed several friends, including Urist, asking if they wanted to see the movie *Lost in Translation* together. Then he e-mailed the group again, this time excluding Sarah, warning them not to come. This ensured he could be alone with Urist. The two continued to date, but Urist soon ended things. According to Green, he was awkward and had trouble talking to this beautiful and intelligent woman who interested him so much. Urist thought he was trying too hard.

The two remained friends, however, and eventually their relationship developed into a romantic one. By this time, not only had *Looking for Alaska* been accepted by a publisher, but Green's second novel had been purchased as well, and it wasn't even finished. Green proposed to Urist in Chicago and moved with her to New York City, where she was attending a two-year master's program at Columbia University. They were married in Birmingham, Alabama, in the spring of 2006.

John Green's twenties had taken him on a road of twists and turns, of peaks and valleys. Now, with two novels under his belt and a new wife on his arm, he felt more stable and secure. But he couldn't have been ready for what would happen next.

LOOKING FOR ALASKA

When *Booklist* editor and writer Ilene Cooper agreed to read Green's attempts at writing, she did not know what to expect. From the reviews Green wrote for the journal, Cooper could tell he was intelligent and funny. But until he submitted forty single-spaced pages of ten-point type, which, Green told the *Chicago Tribune*, "looked almost like ramblings of a serial killer," she didn't know what she'd be working with. What she saw was very raw and lacked shape, but she was impressed with Green's original voice.

She acted as Green's editor, establishing deadlines and suggesting he reconsider the way he told the story. Green told the *Tribune*, "She taught me everything about structure. She used to talk about the shapes of novels: With *Alaska*, you have to start out with this initial event of this kid going to boarding school, and you have to spiral it out from there, but you always have to be circling something that happens at that initial moment. And that was a really helpful way for me to think about it."

And then, they agreed Green's story was ready to be seen. Using her contacts in the publishing industry, Cooper sent off the manuscript to an editor she knew. That editor loved it, and, after a few more rounds of revision, *Looking for Alaska* was published by Dutton Children's Books (a division of Penguin) in March 2005. In his acknowledgements, Green thanks Cooper, his "fairy godmother."

THE STORY

Green was lucky to find such a helpful and dedicated mentor. Many first-time authors run into obstacles because they are trying to achieve a balance between writing what they know and maintaining an objective perspective about their story.

Although Green has said that *Looking for Alaska* is the most autobiographical of his novels, its readers should not mistake the novel for a memoir. *Looking for Alaska* tells the story of Miles Halter, a friendless high schooler who decides he needs to make a change in his life. He transfers to Culver Creek boarding school in another state,

Green's characters are authentic and wholly believable. He is able to avoid two common traps: patronizing his audience and writing teen characters that act like adults.

hoping to pursue the "Great Perhaps," a phrase used by Renaissance writer François Rabelais to mean a future of possibilities. Miles doesn't know what he'll find, but he is driven to seek it.

Once there, Miles falls in with a small but intelligent and rebellious fringe group. For the first time, he feels as if he is a part of something. They study together, break the rules together, and ponder life's great questions together. It is an exciting time for Miles, and in many ways, it seems this is where he begins to live the life he's been seeking.

One member of the group, a moody but charismatic young woman named Alaska, changes Miles's life. She connects him with his first girlfriend, which leads to his first sexual experience, even as she flirts with him and he falls in love with her. She is also unpredictable and sometimes pushes him away.

Miles also becomes interested in academics, particularly a religion course taught by a wise and symbolic character known as the "Old Man." Through this course, and through the Old Man's challenges, Miles explores universal questions he has never pondered before, all part of his journey to the "Great Perhaps."

The novel climaxes with a horrifying tragedy that stuns Miles and his friends. The tragedy brings up a host of philosophical and theological questions for Miles, who must learn that sometimes our greatest questions do not get answered. Though they may never get over their loss, they learn that they need to lean on each other and keep living. Miles begins to understand that the "Great Perhaps" will be more complex and unpredictable than he could ever have imagined.

RECEPTION TO THE NOVEL

Green has commented on how the novel changed over the course of the lengthy revision process. In her initial development sessions with Green, Cooper encouraged him to change

Looking for Alaska was favorably compared to The Catcher in the Rye, a classic coming-of-age novel written by one of Green's heroes, J. D. Salinger.

the novel's structure, which he'd originally written to jump around in time. Cooper believed the story needed to be told linearly. She also suggested that Green use the tragic event as a time marker so that in Miles's mind, everything can be measured in days before and after it, much like we reference time using BCE and CE.

Upon publication, *Looking for Alaska* garnered positive reviews, including many that were starred and recommended. Several compared Miles Halter to one of Green's literary heroes, Holden Caulfield. *Publisher's Weekly* wrote, "Readers will only hope that this is not the last word from this promising new author."

And then the awards rolled in. *Looking for Alaska* made the year-end best-of lists from many reputable review journals, including *Kirkus Reviews*, *Booklist*, and *School Library Journal*. It was a finalist for the *Los Angeles Times* Book Prize and the winner of the 2005 Michael L. Printz Award. This award is presented by the American Library Association. It honors the literary merit of books written for young adults.

CONTROVERSY SURROUNDS THE NOVEL

Along with the accolades came controversy. While *Looking for Alaska* was praised by many for its honest

THE ROLE OF AN EDITOR

When Green's novel was acquired by Dutton Children's Books, he was assigned to editor Julie Strauss-Gabel. The two continue to work together to this day. In one Vlogbrothers video, Green addresses the role Julie plays in the development of his novels:

> I think the assumption that editors exist primarily to fix grammar errors is really incorrect. I mean, I could just read the University of Chicago style manual, I don't need Julie for that. ... But I also think it's incorrect when people think the main reason editors exist is to censor your work or to somehow make it worse. Without Julie, *Paper Towns* would be devoted largely not to Walt Whitman's "Song of Myself" but to an incredibly boring history of the machinations of the United States Postal Service. And without Julie, instead of Colin and Hassan hunting for feral hogs in rural Tennessee, there would be this seventy-five-page—and I'm not making this up—how-to guide about how to take a roadkilled raccoon, skin it, and then tan its hide. ... And without Julie—and before her my amazing mentor and first editor Ilene Cooper—nothing that anyone likes about *Looking for Alaska* would be in that book. ...While God knows I'd like to think that writers are more important than editors, the truth is that we may not be.

portrayal of its teen characters, others—mostly parents of teenagers—viewed it as inappropriate reading for young adults. The book was added to the English

When high schools banned *Looking for Alaska*, Green could not stand by idly. He believes strongly that young adults are mature enough to understand complex and sophisticated works of art.

literature curriculum of many schools, and some parents objected to what they considered explicit material in the book.

In one particular case, a school near Buffalo, New York, gave parents the option of allowing their eleventh-graders to read the book for class. The students who weren't granted permission would simply read a different book. Although this seemed a reasonable compromise, a group of disapproving parents and other members of the community fought to get the book banned altogether. Because *Looking for Alaska* contains incidents of smoking, drinking, and swearing, as well as one scene with sexual content, they deemed it "pornography."

Green wrote a letter in support of the school, and he encouraged his fans to do the same. In a video blog, he states his position eloquently and forcefully. To those who think teenagers are not equipped to understand sophisticated content, he counters,

> Stop condescending to teenagers. Do you seriously think that teenagers aren't able to read critically? When they read George Orwell's *Animal Farm* do they head out to the pig farms to kill all the pigs because they're about to become communist autocrats? When they read *Huck Finn* do they think that Huck should turn Jim in because the demented conscience of the community says so?

It wasn't that Green was insisting that his book be part of the school's curriculum; but on principle he vehemently disagrees with the notion of banning books because teenagers might not be able to handle them. And even more than that, Green rallies against small, organized groups of book banners that attempt to bully school administrations.

This particular school decided to continue teaching *Looking for Alaska*, thanks to dedicated teachers, administration, teen readers, and the book's own author.

While many authors struggle through their first few novels to find an audience, John Green found success with his debut. *Looking for Alaska* allowed him to focus full-time on a future as a writer.

A BRIGHT FUTURE

Green was now a published novelist. But even better, he was an acclaimed and decorated author. To receive such attention and respect for a debut novel is rare and unexpected. Through hard work and perseverance, Green had accomplished something he always believed was beyond his grasp.

The book sold well enough that he felt he could quit his job at *Booklist*. This made it easier to embark on the book tour set up by his publisher. Green was aware that he probably still needed to be employed beyond writing novels, so he joined the staff of *Mental Floss* magazine. *Mental Floss* is a magazine full of fun and interesting facts. In other words, it is something that Green's future protagonist Colin Singleton from *An Abundance of Katherines* might read.

A YOUNG ADULT NOVELIST

While Green was working with Julie Strauss-Gabel during the long process of revising *Looking for Alaska*, he was also writing what would become his second novel, *An Abundance of Katherines*. In fact, Dutton had acquired Green's next work before it was even finished.

AN ABUNDANCE OF KATHERINES

Green had been moved to write *Katherines* after breaking up with a girlfriend. Feeling like a failure at relationships, he realized that he had been dumped more than fifty times. This inspired the character of Colin Singleton, who obsessively charts his

Green is pictured here in Amsterdam, where he traveled while writing portions of *The Fault in Our Stars*, his most popular novel to date.

relationships with ex-girlfriends, all of whom are named Katherine. And just as Colin finds hope and love at the end of the novel, Green broke his dumping streak when he met Sarah Urist, whom he met just before the novel was acquired, and who would become his wife.

Colin is a Chicago teen who has dated and been dumped by nineteen Katherines. He is also a child prodigy who lives in desperate fear of growing older and losing what makes him special. Deciding he needs a break from the pressures of becoming a wash-up and a loser in love, he agrees to embark on a road trip with his best friend, Hassan.

They make it as far as a small town in Tennessee, where they are taken in by the owner of the local plant and her daughter, Lindsay. Heartbroken Colin becomes obsessed with creating an algorithm to predict dumpers and dumpees in romantic relationships, convinced this will prevent him from future heartbreak.

Green sets *Katherines* apart from many YA novels by using footnotes as a literary device. Since Colin's brain is filled with facts and anagrams, Green includes footnotes to further explain the things Colin knows. Green was in part inspired by one of his favorite novels, David Foster Wallace's *Infinite Jest*, which famously features pages upon pages of complicated and humorous footnotes. On his web page,

Green explains, "Sometimes exceptionally intelligent people [like Colin] feel this need to qualify and refine and analyze everything they say, because they feel this urge to be both understood and intellectually precise. Footnotes can serve as a way of attempting to achieve that precision and clarity."

An Abundance of Katherines was selected as a Michael L. Printz Honor book. It also was named among the best books of the year by *Booklist*, *Horn Book*, and *Kirkus*, as well as a finalist for the *Los Angeles Times* Book Prize.

PAPER TOWNS

Green's third novel, a mystery, was published in 2008. By then Green and Urist had moved to Indianapolis, Indiana, where Urist was working as curator of contemporary art at the Indianapolis Museum of Art. Based on the popularity of his previous novels and positive advance reviews, *Paper Towns* debuted in the number five slot on the prestigious *New York Times* best-seller list for children's books. It would go on to win the Edgar Award for Best Young Adult Mystery.

The protagonist of *Paper Towns* is Quentin Jacobsen, who along with his friends is bullied by the popular students in their suburban Orlando, Florida, high school. His childhood friend, Margo

John Green's novels have been translated into many languages and are international best sellers. Green was awarded with the Corine 2010 Young Reader's Award for *Paper Towns*.

Roth Spiegelman, whom he worships even though she became popular, disappears one day, leaving Quentin to search for clues. Quentin's quest forces him to understand who Margo really is and brings him slightly closer to the bullies.

Green addresses two very important themes in *Paper Towns*. One is bullying. Green has commented that he was bullied during his childhood.

In a powerful video on his YouTube channel, Green notes that while, as a bullied kid, all he wanted to do was exact revenge on those who had hurt him, he later understood that being bullied wasn't about him at all. He realized that the kids bullying him often had deep problems of their own.

He also debunks a troubling literary archetype. In the character of Margo, Green dispels the

ROAD TRIPS

John Green's novels share many commonalities, but one of the more interesting is his use of the road trip. In *An Abundance of Katherines*, it's a way for Colin to escape from the pressures of life. Quentin and his friends take one in *Paper Town*s to find Margo, but also for adventure. What is it about the road trip that makes Green feature it in his novels? He explains on his website,

> Road trips are a good example of a thing we all do in our real lives that is a metaphorical action. When you go on a road trip, you are not only hoping that your geography will change: You're hoping that the literal journey will be accompanied by an emotional or spiritual journey, and that you will come home different. So I think I keep returning to them because as a teenager, road trips were one of the places where metaphor was real and alive and relevant to me.

"manic pixie dream girl." This archetype describes a female character who is desperately adored by a male protagonist for no good reason except that she is beautiful and mysterious but quirky and often troubled. The manic pixie dream girl is criticized because she does not have qualities of a real, live woman.

At first, Quentin worships Margo because she is a beautiful enigma. However, eventually he realizes that all of the qualities he had projected onto her do not fit. As Green writes on his website, "I wanted to write a mystery in which the obstacle was ultimately that one character (Quentin) has so profoundly and consistently misimagined another character (Margo) that he can't find her–not because she's hard to find but because in a sense he's looking for the wrong person."

WILL GRAYSON, WILL GRAYSON

Green's next novel, published in 2010, was a departure from his previous efforts. *Will Grayson, Will Grayson* is a collaboration with young adult author David Levithan, perhaps best known for cowriting *Nick and Norah's Infinite Playlist* with Rachel Cohn. *Will Grayson, Will Grayson* debuted on the *New York Times* best-seller list for children's books.

Green's Will Grayson is a frustrated teenager from Chicago who thinks he hates his best friend,

David Levithan *(above)* and John Green cowrote *Will Grayson, Will Grayson*, a novel about two boys with the same name. The experience changed Green's writing process.

the charismatic Tiny Cooper, who happens to be gay. In defending his friend, Will has become a social pariah at school. It takes him most of the book to understand how special Tiny is and to appreciate their friendship.

Will's namesake is a bitter teenager from Ohio who lives with his single mother. This Will is gay and spends his free time in chat rooms but doesn't open up to anyone at school about it, especially his annoying friend Maura, whom he knows is desperately in love with him. In a twist of events, Will Grayson ends up meeting Will Grayson, and the result is that they both learn to open up and expose their true selves, even if it means risking heartbreak.

Green and Levithan decided to write alternating chapters, with the idea that their protagonists would share a name and meet up at some point. Although they were responsible for writing their respective chapters, they did agree on plot points together, and they spent years revising their manuscript to make sure the chapters and characters came together seamlessly. Revising the manuscript was quite a change for Green, who normally changes a high percentage of content from draft to draft. He could not do that without affecting Levithan, and thus he was forced to change his process in a way he found gratifying.

The novel spent three weeks on the *New York Times* best-seller list. But its publication could not have eclipsed an even more important event that same year: the birth of John and Sarah Green's first child, son Henry, on January 20.

THE WRITING PROCESS

Green is a very disciplined writer, as evidenced by his rather prolific output. Most days, he spends his entire morning (and sometimes longer) writing, using the afternoon hours for other commitments. He also travels a great deal to support his books and other projects.

Inspiration does not come from a major concept that falls into his lap. Rather, it may be the faint lines of a character or an idea he's been kicking around for years. The important thing for him is to get something down on the page and not worry about it being perfect. During the revision process, he throws out a major percentage of his first draft, so he does not pressure himself to come up with perfection right out of the gate.

Green's advice to aspiring writers is to read as much as possible and as broadly as possible. Another thing Green credits in helping his storytelling is simply talking to friends. When you tell stories to your friends, you see what interests them as well as what bores them, and you get a knack for what people want to hear.

Sometimes Green gets midway through a novel and realizes it's not a story he wants to tell. He must make the difficult decision to abandon the writing, but he tries to look at that as a learning experience. And he never knows when he might use something from that writing in the future.

It may surprise fans of his books that John Green is usually disappointed with his work. After a time, he packs his novels away in his mind and doesn't really think about them anymore. This is a necessary part of the process because by this time he is working on one or two new novels.

Green trusts that once he has finished a novel, it becomes the readers'. As an author, he doesn't want to get in the way of a reader's experience with his book. And while he is happy to answer many other questions from his readers, he will never imagine for them what happens to a character after the novel ends.

FIVE

THE FAULT IN OUR STARS

The relationship between books and their readers was actually one of the subjects on Green's mind when he wrote *The Fault in Our Stars*, which was published in 2012. For this novel, arguably Green's finest to date, the author made use of some past writing failures, including what he calls "the sequel" and the "desert island book."

He was also finally ready to use in a direct way the experience he had gained working as a student chaplain all those years ago. Green had been struggling to write about sick children for a decade, but his efforts always fell flat. This changed when he attended LeakyCon, a conference for fans of the Harry Potter series in 2009.

A STAR NAMED ESTHER

At the conference, he met fifteen-year-old Esther Earl. Esther was a nerdfighter who loved to write and make YouTube videos. She and Green quickly struck up a friendship, which further developed over the Internet. Green found Esther funny, intelligent, and artistic. He also knew that she had cancer.

Green used his experience as a hospital chaplain and inspiration from his friend Esther Earl to write his fifth novel, *The Fault in Our Stars*.

Esther didn't let on to Green or the rest of their Internet community that her cancer was serious. One day, typing back and forth with Green, she mentioned that she was writing from the intensive care unit (ICU). Green quickly learned from her parents that Esther's cancer was terminal.

IS HAZEL ESTHER?

John Green must feel like a broken record, repeating his philosophy that readers should have their own experience with books, rather than focusing on the author's intent. In fact, *The Fault in Our Stars* includes an author's note with this line: "Neither novels or their readers benefit from attempts to divine whether any facts hide inside a story." In spite of this direct request, Green frequently found himself answering a question from readers and interviewers: Is Hazel Lancaster a fictionalized version of Esther Earl?

Green states on his website that Esther is not in the details of Hazel; they share very few specifics other than the terminal thyroid cancer. However, he told *Parade* magazine, Esther inspired Hazel in much larger ways:

> I've said many times that *The Fault in Our Stars*, while it is dedicated to Esther, is not about her. When the book was published, lots of reporters wanted me to talk about Esther; they wanted to know if my book was "based on a true story." I never really knew how to deal with these questions, and I still don't, because the truth (as always) is complicated. Esther inspired the story in the sense that my anger after her death pushed me to write constantly. She helped me to imagine teenagers as more empathetic than I'd given them credit for, and her charm and snark inspired the novel, too, but the character of Hazel is very different from Esther, and Hazel's story is not Esther's. Esther's story belonged to her.

After Esther's death, her parents published a book of her journals and drawings posthumously, called *This Star Won't Go Out*. (Esther means "star.") The introduction was written by her biggest fan, John Green.

This news shocked Green and the rest of Esther's friends. But sharing it actually served to strengthen their relationships. Esther became an important part of the nerdfighter community, helping to raise funds for the Harry Potter Alliance. And that made it even more heartbreaking, not least for Green, when Esther Earl lost her battle to cancer on August 25, 2010.

During his friendship with Esther, Green was still struggling to write about kids with cancer. In fact, he was very conscious of not exploiting their relationship by using her experience in his writings. However, he was so angry about Esther's death that he was compelled to write. He wrote quickly and constantly. And the result is a remarkable novel.

THE STORY

The Fault in Our Stars follows Hazel Lancaster, who is terminally ill with thyroid cancer. Though her doctors have found a medication to keep her alive for the time being, Hazel is painfully aware that she will die soon. This knowledge has given her a sarcastic sense of humor and wisdom beyond her years, but she also worries about the things that occupy other teenagers' minds.

Hazel is cared for by loving parents, a hyper-emotional father and a suffocating mother. At a cancer support group that her mother forces her

The Fault in Our Stars was adapted for the big screen starring *(left to right)* Nat Wolff as Isaac, Shailene Woodley as Hazel, and Ansel Elgort as Augustus.

to attend, she meets a charismatic boy named Augustus "Gus" Waters. A former basketball star, Gus beat bone cancer after losing a leg. Hazel is stunned and disarmed when the handsome boy seems attracted to her.

The two strike up a funny and intense friendship immediately, introducing their favorite things to one another. Gus recommends the novelization of his favorite video game and Hazel has him read a book she is obsessed with, a novel called *An Imperial Affliction*.

Her dream is to meet its reclusive author, Peter Van Houton, who lives in Amsterdam. Before she dies, she needs to ask him what happens to the main character after the book ends. Hazel is obsessed with what happens to characters after books end because she worries about what will become of her parents after she's gone and they are no longer parents, technically.

When Hazel becomes critically ill, Gus uses his wish from support foundation "The Genies" to take her to Amsterdam to meet Peter Van Houton. While in the magical city, the love between Hazel and Gus blossoms.

REACTION TO THE NOVEL

The Fault in Our Stars is a special book in many ways. One is the way in which the book was marketed and sold. By the time he submitted the manuscript to his publisher, Green was a best-selling author of four novels. He had toured and visited many schools to support his books and meet his readers.

He also had a strong presence on social media, including a popular video blog with his brother, Hank, and burgeoning Twitter and Tumblr accounts. He had brought together a network of like-minded

The Fault in Our Stars was named the number one fiction book of the year by *Time*, a remarkable feat for a young-adult novel. Green gained fans of all ages, thanks to the success of the book.

documentaries and the reality series *Pawn Stars* while he signed.

The Fault in Our Stars debuted at number one on the *New York Times* best-seller list for children's books, where it remained for forty-four weeks. It also was a best seller for the *Wall Street Journal*, *Bookseller*, and *IndieBound*, and received starred reviews from *Booklist*, *School Library Journal*, *Publishers Weekly*, *Horn Book*, and *Kirkus Reviews*. In addition, it was a *New York Times* Book Review Editor's Choice book. *Time* magazine named it the number one fiction book of the year, and it made several prestigious "best of the year" compilation lists.

The Fault in Our Stars was so popular that it impacted the sales of Green's past books. *Looking for Alaska*, for example, made the *New York Times* best-seller list for children that summer, seven years after it was published.

THE MOVIE

Not long after, Hollywood came calling. The novel was optioned by 20th Century Fox, and shooting began in summer 2013 in Pittsburgh, Pennsylvania. Although Green was not involved in adapting his beloved novel for the screen, he did spend time on the set and chronicled it in video blogs for nerdfighters.

This success inspired studios to adapt Green's other novels. *Looking for Alaska* had been optioned years earlier, and Paramount Pictures hired a director and screenwriter only weeks after *The Fault in Our Stars* premiered. Also, 20th Century Fox will release a *Paper Towns* film, with Green as an executive producer. *The Fault in Our Stars* movie, by contrast, appears to have been a wonderful experience for him, judging by his funny, often giddy, videos from the set. The movie was released in the United States on June 6, 2014. It took in $48.2 million in its opening weekend, an excellent number considering only $30 million was spent to make it.

DON'T FORGET TO BE AWESOME

Although John Green certainly considers himself an author, writing books for young adults isn't the only job he has. Green describes himself as an introvert, but anyone who has seen him on a book tour or in an Internet video knows that he is a high-energy, intelligent person excited to engage with others. How could someone who fits that description be content to sit alone in a room and write all day?

"When you're writing a novel, you spend four years sitting in your basement and a year waiting for the book to come out and then you get the feedback," Green told the *Los Angeles Times.* "When you do work online, the moment you're finished making it, people start responding to it which is really fun and allows for a kind of

community development you just can't have in novels."

BROTHERHOOD 2.0

In late 2006, Green realized that he and his brother, Hank, were keeping in touch mostly via texts and e-mails. They decided to challenge themselves. For an entire year, beginning New Year's Day 2007, they would stop written communication and start a "conversation" through vlog, or video blog.

They established rules and punishments for infractions. (Punishments for these violations included waxing their chins and legs, eating a blenderized McDonald's Happy Meal, and eating as many Peeps as possible in six minutes.) Hank and John posted the video blogs on their YouTube channel, Vlogbrothers, though they did not expect to have much of an audience.

Midway through the experiment, Hank, a rabid Harry Potter fan, wrote a song about the upcoming film Harry Potter book and

Brothers John and Hank Green became Internet sensations through their social experiment Brotherhood 2.0. The project also brought them closer together.

posted his performance to YouTube. To the brothers' shock, the video received a million views. Suddenly, viewers of the viral video checked out the Vlogbrothers video blogs.

And the next thing the Greens knew, they had their own group of rabid fans. Some had read and loved *Looking for Alaska*; others were Harry Potter fans. And still others just enjoyed their combination of intelligence, humor, and rapid-fire delivery.

Brotherhood 2.0 ended on December 31, 2007, but John and Hank decided to continue with a modified version of the project, beginning in January 2008, which they called the Vlogbrothers. This video blog is less frequent but retains all of the charm of the original. The Vlogbrothers have kept up their YouTube channel for more than five years. In 2013, their channel boasted one million subscribers.

Because they know a thing or two about building a community, in 2010 the brothers founded a professional conference called VidCon. This annual conference brings together creators and viewers of online videos.

NERDFIGHTERS

In his February 17, 2007, Brotherhood 2.0 vlog, John tells Hank that on a recent trip, he spied a video game called *Nerd Fighters* at the Columbus, Ohio, airport. (He had actually misread the game's name, *Hero Fighters.*) They decided that nerdfighters fight for (not against) nerds, for intellectualism, for originality, for being generally awesome, and for trying to make the world a better place.

It was in John's March 5 entry that he first proposed starting a fund for nerdfighters to improve the world. He promised, "We're starting something here, something important. Something that's going to allow us to decrease the overall level of world suck."

By August, he was listing the many accomplishments of nerdfighters, from splintering off into other charity endeavors, to creating arts and crafts inspired by the Green brothers' projects. These included songs, videos, T-shirts, photographs, embroidered pillowcases, and alternate book cover designs.

And that's when it became perfectly clear that this project John and Hank Green had begun on a whim had legs, and that it had inspired more people and taken off in directions they never could have imagined. In his August 29 entry, John reflected on the growing phenomenon and how it had in turn affected him:

> The old-school nerdfighters are doing a great job of integrating all of the new-school nerdfighters so that everyone collectively finds

John Green participated in a fireside chat with President Barack Obama in 2013. Green was selected, in part, because of his presence on social media.

that they are made of more awesome than they ever thought possible. Hank, I don't want to exaggerate the effect that this project is having on my life, but it's sort of starting to make me believe in humanity again. I find myself saying and thinking outlandishly optimistic things lately. ... Maybe the world contains more nerdfighters than nerd haters.

The nerdfighter motto is "Don't Forget to Be Awesome" (DFTBA), and they flash a variation of *Star Trek*'s Vulcan sign as a greeting.

PROJECT FOR AWESOME

On December 17, 2007, Hank announced via vlog that the brothers had a new special project.

John Green and the stars of *The Fault in Our Stars* pose with young fans.

Nerdfighters would be taking over YouTube! Rather than its usual fare of kittens and other distractions, YouTube would be packed with ways to make a difference in the world. The brothers challenged fans to post homemade videos promoting charities they supported. All of the videos would share the same thumbnail so that they would appear as YouTube's top-discussed videos of the day. Nerdfighters posted more than four hundred videos for such diverse organizations as UNICEF, Autism Speaks, the World Wildlife Fund, and Toys for Tots.

This feat was made possible by four thousand nerdfighters, who viewed the videos and voted for their favorites. The end result was that a large group of nerdfighters became aware of, and in many cases donated time and money to,

ELEANOR OR ALICE?

John Green's popularity with young people, not to mention his intelligence and political awareness, made him a natural choice to participate in a fireside chat with President Barack Obama in 2013. Green was selected along with five others proven to have cultivated large fan bases through their strong online presence. Via videoconference, each person was allowed to ask the president several questions. After Green had asked several intelligent questions, he was joined by a visibly pregnant Urist. The Greens asked President Obama if he preferred the name Eleanor or Alice for their baby. The president diplomatically declined to weigh in. However, he cleverly closed his non-answer to the disappointed parents by saying, "Tell either Eleanor or Alice not to forget to be awesome." Could the president be a nerdfighter?

charities they might not have known about. In addition, John and Hank increased their viewership by another thousand.

The Project for Awesome has become an annual event. It has grown in numbers and in influence. The Vlogbrothers' own Foundation to Decrease World Suck now raises funds that are distributed to the five charities that receive the most votes.

Perhaps more than anything they had done thus far, the Project for Awesome proved the brothers' point that, in this age of the Internet, people can band together more than ever and accomplish a goal. The nerdfighters had made great strides toward reducing world suck.

CRASHCOURSE

Because of their massive following as the Vlogbrothers, YouTube approached John and Hank Green to be a part of an exciting new project. Google had given YouTube funding to create one hundred channels of original programming, and many leaders and celebrities, including Madonna, Deepak Chopra, Shaquille O'Neal, and Amy Poehler, signed on to create channels. John and Hank would create a new channel, as well.

The result is CrashCourse. A series of educational videos, the crash courses are hosted by John and Hank and written in conjunction with educators. They include animations, solid facts, and the Vlogbrothers' trademark fast-paced humor. The channel launched in 2012. The courses offered so far have been biology, ecology, chemistry, and psychology from Hank; and world history, U.S. history, and English literature from John. By 2014, the CrashCourse channel had more than one million subscribers.

Due to the success of his novels and his strong Internet presence, John Green is able to draw large crowds. This makes him a rock star of the literary world.

AN EVENING OF AWESOME

To celebrate the one-year anniversary of the publication of *The Fault in Our Stars*, the Vlogbrothers hosted a variety show that they called "An Evening of Awesome." Their intent was to bring together the different communities that had found camaraderie as nerdfighters. The night was also a treat for those who had committed so much to reducing world suck.

On January 15, 2013, nearly three thousand excited fans packed into the hall for the sold-out show. Those who couldn't get tickets watched a live broadcast on YouTube. Green's publisher, Penguin, partnered with Tumblr for the event, with many bookstores and libraries hosting watch parties.

That night, Carnegie Hall was the number one trending topic on Twitter. Green said of the nerdfighter community he was instrumental in bringing together, "It has helped me fall in love with the world."

CONNECTING WITH THE WORLD

John Green began his career by simply wanting to tell a story. That story turned into four best-selling novels that have helped young adults find a literary voice they can connect with. But it wasn't enough for Green to write in a vacuum and hear from his fans after each novel was published. He wanted a stronger, more immediate connection.

Green's willingness to avail himself to his fans and to other like-minded people resulted in a bigger, more diverse community. Along with his brother, Hank, he has proven that it is cool to be a nerd, that being smart will take you far in life, and that we all can make a difference in the world.

He has changed the face of publishing and traveled the open road of the Internet. His appearances on YouTube have helped make him a star and so much more. As he says on his website:

If it weren't for YouTube, I wouldn't be best friends with my brother. I wouldn't have the words "*New York Times* best-selling author" associated with my name. I wouldn't have a way to join forces with other people and pool our resources to build huge water filters for villages in Bangladesh, and I wouldn't be able to meet those villagers over video and come to know and care about them as people and not just two-dimensional images of poverty.

Just another step on John Green's "Great Perhaps."

FACT SHEET ON JOHN GREEN

Born: August 24, 1977

Current Residence: Indianapolis, Indiana

Education: Kenyon College: B.A. English/Religious Studies

First Publication: *Looking for Alaska* (2005)

Family: Sarah Urist Green, wife

Henry Green, son

Alice Green, daughter

Hank Green, brother

Side Jobs: YouTube vlogger; VidCon cofounder; CrashCourse creator

FACT SHEET ON JOHN GREEN'S WORK

Looking for Alaska

New York, NY: Dutton Children's Books, 2005

Plot Summary: Miles Halter is fascinated by famous last words—and tired of his safe life at home. He leaves for boarding school to seek what the dying poet Francois Rabelais called the "Great Perhaps." Much awaits Miles at Culver Creek, including Alaska Young. Clever, funny, screwed-up, and dead sexy, Alaska will pull Miles into her labyrinth and catapult him into the Great Perhaps.

Awards: Winner, 2006 Michael L. Printz Award

Finalist, 2005 *Los Angeles Times* Book Prize

2006 Top 10 Best Book for Young Adults

2006 Teens' Top 10 Award

2006 Quick Pick for Reluctant Young Adult Readers

A New York Public Library Book for the Teen Age

A *Booklist* Editor's Choice Pick

Barnes & Noble Discover Great New Writers Selection

Borders Original Voices Selection
Translated into more than fifteen languages

An Abundance of Katherines
New York, NY: Dutton Children's Books, 2006
Plot Summary: When it comes to relationships,
everyone has a type. Colin Singleton's type is
girls named Katherine. He has dated—and been
dumped by nineteen Katherines. In the wake of
the K–19 Debacle, Colin—an anagram-obsessed
washed-up child prodigy—heads out on a road
trip with his overweight, Judge Judy-loving friend
Hassan. With $10,000 in his pocket and a feral
hog on his trail, Colin is on a mission to prove a
mathematical theorem that he hopes will predict
the future of any relationship (and conceivably
win the girl).
Awards: 2007 Michael L. Printz Honor book
Los Angeles Times Book Prize finalist
Booklist book of the year
Horn Book book of the year
Kirkus book of the year

Paper Towns
New York, NY: Dutton Children's Books, 2008
Plot Summary: Quentin Jacobsen has spent a
lifetime loving the magnificently adventurous

Margo Roth Spiegelman from afar. So when she cracks open a window and climbs back into his life—dressed like a ninja and summoning him for an ingenious campaign of revenge—he follows. After their all-nighter ends and a new day breaks, Q arrives at school to discover that Margo, always an enigma, has disappeared. But Q soon learns that there are clues–and they're for him. Urged down a disconnected path, the closer he gets, the less Q sees of the girl he thought he knew.

Awards: Winner, 2009 Edgar Award for Best Young Adult Mystery

Debuted at number five on the *New York Times* best-seller list for children's books

Will Grayson, Will Grayson
New York, NY: Dutton Children's Books, 2010

Plot Summary: One cold night, in a most unlikely corner of Chicago, two teens—both named Will Grayson—are about to cross paths. As their worlds collide and intertwine, the Will Graysons find their lives going in new and unexpected directions, building toward romantic turns-of-heart and the epic production of history's most fabulous high school musical.

Awards: Debuted at number three on the *New York Times* best-seller list for children's books, the first book starring gay characters ever to appear on the list.

The Fault in Our Stars
New York, NY: Dutton Children's Books, 2012

Plot Summary: Despite the tumor-shrinking medical miracle that has bought her a few years, Hazel has never been anything but terminal, her final chapter inscribed upon diagnosis. But when a gorgeous plot twist named Augustus Waters suddenly appears at support group for kids with cancer, Hazel's story is about to be completely rewritten.

Awards: Debuted at number one on the *New York Times* best-seller list for children's books.

A movie adaptation was released in 2014.

Looking for Alaska

"Green…has a writer's voice, so self-assured and honest that one is startled to learn that this novel is his first. The anticipated favorable comparisons to Holden Caufield are richly deserved in this highly recommended addition to young adult literature." —*VOYA*

"Like Phineas in John Knowles' 'A Separate Peace,' Green draws Alaska so lovingly, in self-loathing darkness as well as energetic light, that readers mourn her loss along with her friends." —*School Library Journal*, starred review

"The spirit of Holden Caulfield lives on." —*KLIATT*

An Abundance of Katherines

"Imagine an operating room at the start of a daring but well-rehearsed procedure and you will have something of the atmosphere of 'An Abundance of Katherines': every detail considered, the action unrolling with grace and inevitability." —*New York Times* Book Review

"Green follows his Printz winning *Looking for Alaska* (2005) with another sharp, intelligent story. The laugh-out-loud humor ranges from delightfully sophomoric to subtly intellectual." —*Booklist*, Starred Review

"Fully fun, challengingly complex, and entirely entertaining." —*Kirkus*, starred review

"Laugh-out-loud funny, this second novel by the author of the Printz winner *Looking for Alaska* charts a singular coming-of-age American road trip that is at once a satire of and a tribute to its many celebrated predecessors." —*Horn Book*, starred review

Paper Towns

"Green's prose is astounding—from hilarious, hyper-intellectual trash talk and shtick, to complex philosophizing, to devastating observation and truths. He nails it—exactly how a thing feels, looks, affects—page after page." —Johanna Lewis, *School Library Journal*, starred review

"A suspenseful mystery, a compelling central metaphor, and one of those road trips that every senior hopes he or she will have round out this exploration of the kind of relationship that can't help but teach us a little bit about ourselves." —Bulletin for the Center of Children's Books, starred review

"A powerfully great read." —*VOYA*

"There are echoes of Green's award-winning *Looking for Alaska* (2005): a lovely, eccentric girl; a mystery that begs to be solved by clever, quirky teens; and telling quotations (from *Leaves of Grass*, this time) beautifully integrated into the plot. Yet, if anything, the thematic stakes are higher here, as Green ponders the interconnectedness of imagination and perception, of mirrors and windows, of illusion and reality. That he brings it off is testimony to the fact that he is not only clever and wonderfully witty but also deeply thoughtful and insightful. In addition, he's a superb stylist, with a voice perfectly matched to his amusing, illuminating material." —Michael Cart, *Booklist*, starred review

Will Grayson, Will Grayson

"A terrific high-energy tale of teen love, lust, intrigue, anger, pain, and friendship threaded with generous measures of comedy." —*Booklist*, starred review

"This quirky yet down-to-earth collaboration by two master YA storytellers will keep readers turning pages." —*School Library Journal*, starred review

"An intellectually existential, electrically ebullient love story that brilliantly melds the ridiculous with the realistic." —*Kirkus*, starred review

"The spectacular style that readers have come to expect from these two YA masters." —*VOYA*

The Fault in Our Stars

"Green's best and most ambitious novel to date. In its every aspect, *The Fault in Our Stars* is a triumph." —*Booklist*, starred review

"Luminous." —*Entertainment Weekly*

"A smartly crafted intellectual explosion of a romance." —*Kirkus*, starred review

"A blend of melancholy, sweet, philosophical, and funny. Green shows us true love…and it is far more romantic than any sunset on the beach." —*New York Times* Book Review

"One doesn't like to throw around phrases like 'instant classic' lightly, but I can see *The Fault in Our Stars* taking its place alongside *Are You There God? It's Me, Margaret* in the young-adult canon. Green's book is also a good example of why so many adult readers are turning to young-adult literature for the pleasures and consolations they used to get from conventional literary fiction." —*Time*

"Green writes books for young adults, but his voice is so compulsively readable that it defies categorization. *The Fault in Our Stars* proves that the hype surrounding Green is not overblown." —*NPR*

"A pitch-perfect, elegiac comedy…it will linger long and hard in the minds of teens and former teens." —*USA Today*

"An achingly beautiful story." —*SLJ*, starred review

"John Green deftly mixes the profound and the quotidian in this tough, touching valentine to the human spirit." —*Washington Post*

August 24, 1977 John Michael Green born in Indianapolis, Indiana.

May 5, 1980 Brother, William Henry "Hank" Green, born.

1995 Graduates from Indian Springs School.

2000 Graduates from Kenyon College, with majors in English and religious studies.

2000 Begins work as hospital chaplain.

2001 Moves to Chicago, Illinois, and works for *Booklist*.

2002 Brings first full draft of *Looking for Alaska* to Ilene Cooper.

2002 Begins contributing essays to Chicago Public Radio.

2005 *Looking for Alaska* published.

2005 Begins working at *Mental Floss.*

2006 Marries Sarah Urist.

2006 *An Abundance of Katherines* published.

January 1, 2007 Begins Brotherhood 2.0 with Hank Green.

2008 The Vlogbrothers rolls out.

2008 *Paper Towns* published.

2009 Meets Esther Earl at a Harry Potter fan conference.

January 20, 2010 Son, Henry, is born.

August 25, 2010 Esther Earl dies.

2010 *Will Grayson, Will Grayson* published.

2012 CrashCourse debuts on YouTube.

2012 *The Fault in Our Stars* published.

January 15, 2013 "An Evening of Awesome" entertains a sold-out crowd at Carnegie Hall.

June 3, 2013 Daughter, Alice, is born.

June 6, 2014 *The Fault in Our Stars* movie released in theaters.

ACCOLADE Praise.

ACQUIRE To locate and purchase a manuscript for publication.

ARCHETYPE The model for a type of character.

CAMARADERIE Spirit and friendship among a group.

CHAPLAIN Clergyperson who conducts religious services for a secular institution.

CHARISMA Magnetism or charm.

COLLEAGUE A professional associate.

COMING-OF-AGE NOVEL A story of a person becoming an adult.

CONCEIT Theme or idea.

CRUCIFORM Taking the shape of a cross.

CURRICULUM Courses offered by a school.

DEFER To delay.

DISCERNMENT The process of understanding something.

DIVINITY The formal study of religion.

DRAFT A version of a manuscript.

ENIGMA A mysterious person who is difficult to understand.

EXPLICIT Containing objectionable material, such as nudity, violence, or sex.

EXPLOITING To use in a way that unfairly helps someone.

FIRESIDE CHAT An informal speech by the U.S. president.

HEADMASTER The head of a private school.

INSULAR Not knowing or being interested in cultures outside one's own.

INTROVERT A person who is shy.

LINEARLY Telling a story in a straightforward sequence of events.

MANIC PIXIE DREAM GIRL An undeveloped female character who is the object of affection of a story's hero.

MANUSCRIPT The form of a book before it is printed.

MONOTONOUS Boring and always the same.

NERDFIGHTER Fans of John and Hank Green whose mission is to decrease world suck.

OPTION To acquire exclusive rights to adapt a novel as a motion picture.

PERSEVERANCE Continued attempts to achieve, in spite of obstacles.

PORTRAYAL Representation.

POSTHUMOUS After death.

PROLIFIC Producing a large volume.

PROTAGONIST Main character.

REDEMPTION Being saved from sin.

REVISION The process of changing and improving a manuscript.

THEOLOGICAL Having to do with religion.

TRANSIENCE The state of not lasting a long time.

UNATTAINABLE Unable to be reached or achieved.

VENUE A place where events are held.

VLOG Video blog.

VORACIOUSLY Eagerly and hungrily.

American Library Association (ALA)
50 East Huron Street
Chicago, IL 60611-2795
(800) 545-2433
Website: http://www.ala.org
ALA is the oldest and largest library association in
the world, providing association information,
news, events, and advocacy resources for members, librarians, and library users.

Booklist
American Library Association
50 East Huron Street
Chicago, IL 60611
Website: http://www.booklistonline.com
Booklist is a book-review magazine that has been published by the American Library Association for more
than a hundred years and is widely viewed as offer-
ing the most reliable reviews to help libraries decide
what to buy and help library patrons and students
decide what to read, view, or listen to.

Canadian Library Association (CLA)
1150 Morrison Drive, Suite 400
Ottawa, ON K2H 8S9
Canada
(613) 232-9625
Website: http://www.cla.ca

CLA is the national voice for Canada's library communities. Its members champion library values and the value of libraries, influence public policy impacting libraries, inspire and support member learning, and collaborate to strengthen the library community.

CLA Young Adult Book Award
1150 Morrison Drive, Suite 400
Ottawa, ON K2H 8S9
Canada
(613) 232-9625
Website: http://www.cla.ca
This award recognizes an author of an outstanding English-language Canadian book that appeals to young adults between the ages of thirteen and eighteen. The award is given annually, when merited, at the Canadian Library Association's annual conference.

Foundation to Decrease World Suck
Missoula, MT 59807
Website: http://www.fightworldsuck.org
The Foundation to Decrease World Suck, is 100 percent volunteer-operated and exists solely for the purpose of raising funds to be donated to other nonprofit organizations. The majority of fund-raising is done through and during the annual Project for Awesome.

Freedom to Read Foundation (FTRF)
50 East Huron Street
Chicago, IL 60611
(800) 545-2433 ext. 4226
Website: http://www.ftrf.org
FTRF is a non-profit legal and educational organization
affiliated with the American Library Association. It
protects and defends the First Amendment to the
U. S. Constitution and supports the right of libraries
to collect—and individuals to access—information.

Harry Potter Alliance
P.O. Box 441640
Somerville, MA 02144
Website: http://thehpalliance.org
The Harry Potter Alliance nonprofit organization
uses parallels from the Harry Potter books to
educate and mobilize young people across the
world toward issues of literacy, equality, and
human rights. Its mission is to empower its
members to act like the heroes that they love
by acting for a better world.

School Library Journal
160 Varick Street, 11th Floor
New York, NY 10013
(646) 380-0700
Website: http://www.slj.com

School Library Journal aspires to be an accelerator for innovation in schools and public libraries that serve the information, literacy, and technology needs of twenty-first-century children and young adults. It produces resources, services, and reviews that make library and education professionals savvier, and communities stronger.

This Star Won't Go Out Foundation (TSWGO)
118 Billings Street
Quincy, MA 02171
Website: http://www.tswgo.org
TSWGO is making a difference in the lives of children with cancer, one family at a time. By providing funds to help pay for travel, a mortgage or rent check, and other cost of living expenses, it frees up families to focus on their child who is in treatment.

VidCon
Anaheim Convention Center
800 W. Katella Avenue
Anaheim, CA 92802
Website: http://www.vidcon.com
VidCon has established itself as the world's premier gathering of people who make online videos, whether they're just starting or have been doing it for years. For the millions who love online

videos, VidCon is the one chance a year to celebrate this new world IRL (in real life).

Young Adult Library Services Association (YALSA)
50 East Huron Street
Chicago, IL 60611-2795
(800) 545-2433
Website: http://www.ala.org
YALSA is a national association of librarians, library workers, and advocates whose mission is to expand and strengthen library services for teens aged twelve to eighteen. It awards the Michael L. Printz Award, an annual prize for a book that exemplifies literary excellence In young adult literature.

WEBSITES

Because of the changing nature of Internet links, Rosen Publishing has developed an online list of websites related to the subject of this book. This site is updated regularly. Please use this link to access the list:

http://www.rosenlinks.com/AAA/Green

Bacigalupi, Paolo. *Ship Breaker.* New York, NY: Little, Brown and Company, 2010.

Cart, Michael. *Young Adult Literature: From Romance to Realism.* Chicago, IL: American Library Association, 2010.

Earl, Esther, with Lori and Wayne Earl. *This Star Won't Go Out: The Life and Words of Esther Grace Earl.* New York, NY: Dutton Children's Books, 2014.

Green, John. *An Abundance of Katherines.* New York, NY: Dutton Children's Books, 2006.

Green, John. "The Approximate Cost of Loving Caroline." In *Twice Told: Original Stories Inspired by Original Art.* New York, NY: Dutton Children's Books, 2006.

Green, John. *The Fault in Our Stars.* New York, NY: Dutton Children's Books, 2012.

Green, John. "Freak the Geek." In *Geektastic*, edited by Holly Black and Cecil Castellucci. New York, NY: Little, Brown and Company, 2009.

Green, John. "The Great American Morp." In *21 Proms*, edited by David Levithan and David Ehrenhaft. New York, NY: Scholastic, 2007.

Green, John, Maureen Johnson, and Lauren Myracle. *Let It Snow: Three Holiday Romances.* New York, NY: Speak, 2008.

Green, John. *Looking for Alaska.* New York, NY: Dutton Children's Books, 2005.

Green, John, Will Pearson, and Mangesh Hattikudur, eds. *Mental Floss: Genius Instruction Manual.* New York, NY: HarperCollins, 2006.

Green, John, Will Pearson, and Mangesh Hattikudur, ed. *Mental Floss: What's the Difference?* New York, NY: HarperCollins, 2006.

Green, John. *Paper Towns.* New York, NY: Dutton Children's Books, 2008.

Green, John, and David Levithan. *Will Grayson, Will Grayson.* New York, NY: Dutton Children's Books, 2010.

Lake, Nick. *In Darkness.* New York, NY: Bloomsbury Children's Books, 2012.

Morrison, Toni. *Song of Solomon.* New York, NY: Knopf, 1977.

Morrison, Toni. *Sula.* New York, NY: Knopf, 1973.

Riggs, Ransom, Will Pearson, Mangesh Hattikudur, and John Green, eds. *Mental Floss: Scatterbrained.* New York, NY: HarperCollins, 2006.

Riggs, Ransom. *Miss Peregrine's Home for Peculiar Children.* Philadelphia, PA: Quirk Books, 2011.

Salinger, J. D. *The Catcher in the Rye.* Boston, MA: Little, Brown and Company, 1951.

Salinger, J. D. *Franny and Zooey.* Boston, MA: Little, Brown and Company, 1961.

Salinger, J. D. *Nine Stories.* Boston, MA: Little, Brown and Company, 1953.

Sedgwick, Marcus. *Midwinterblood*. New York, NY: Roaring Brook Press, 2013.

Smith, Zadie. *White Teeth*. New York, NY: Random House, 2000.

Wallace, David Foster. *Infinite Jest: A Novel.* Boston, MA: Little, Brown and Company, 1996.

Whaley, John Corey. *Where Things Come Back.* New York, NY: Atheneum Books for Young Readers, 2011.

Zusak, Markus. *The Book Thief*. Sydney, Australia: Picador, 2005.

"August 20th: Winner, South Dakota." YouTube video, 3:37, by Vlogbrothers, August 20, 2007. Retrieved December 2013 (http://www.youtube.com/watch?v=NzHqq4RQhDA).

Barnes, Brooks. "Teenage Angst Trumps Sci-Fi at the Box Office." *New York Times*, June 8, 2014.

Brison-Trezise, Gabe. "Admissions Flaunts Green, but Some See Strategy as Limiting." *Kenyon Collegian*, November 14, 2013. Retrieved December 2014 (http://www.kenyoncollegian.com/news/admissions-flaunts-green-but-some-see-strategy-as-limiting-1.3119116#.Uu0VPPZNcy5).

"Brotherhood 2.0: March 5, 2007: Hank's Punishment." YouTube video, 2:46, by Vlogbrothers, March 5, 2007. Accessed January 2014 (http://www.youtube.com/watch?v=57LN_AerTM4).

Carpenter, Susan. "John Green's Adds to His Fan Base with 'The Fault in Our Stars.'" *Los Angeles Times*, January 21, 2012. Retrieved December 2013 (http://articles.latimes.com/2012/jan/21/entertainment/la-et-john-green-20120121).

Castellitto, Linda M. "John Green: A Signature Move Pays Off for John Green." BookPage.com, January 2012. Retrieved December 2013 (http://

bookpage.com/interviews/8768-john-green#
.Uu0wx_ZNcy5).

Chang, Jade. "Interview with John Green."
Goodreads.com, December 2012. Retrieved
December 2013 (http://www.goodreads.com/
interviews/show/828.John_Green).

Goodnow, Cecelia. "John Green Isn't Just a
Prize-Winning Author, He's Also a YouTube Cutup."
Seattle Post-Intelligencer, October 27, 2008.
Retrieved November 2013 (http://www.seattlepi
.com/ae/books/article/John-Green-isn-t-just-a
-prize-winning-author-1289576.php).

Green, John. "An Abundance of Katherines."
JohnGreenBooks.com. Retrieved December
2013 (http://johngreenbooks.com/katherines).

Green, John. "Biographical Questions."
JohnGreenBooks.com. Retrieved October
2013 (http://johngreenbooks.com/
biographical-questions).

Green, John. "FAQ." JohnGreenBooks.com.
Retrieved October 2013 (http://johngreenbooks
.com/faq).

Green, John. "The Fault in Our Stars."
JohnGreenBooks.com. Retrieved December
2013 http://johngreenbooks.com/the-fault-in
-our-stars).

Green, John. *The Fault in Our Stars.* New York,
NY: Dutton Children's Books, 2012.

Green, John. "Looking for Alaska." JohnGreenBooks
.com. Retrieved December 2013 (http://
johngreenbooks.com/looking-for-alaska).

Green, John. "Nick." JohnGreenBooks.com. May
26, 2003. Retrieved November 2013 (http://
johngreenbooks.com/nick-from-all-things
-considered).

Green, John. "Paper Towns." JohnGreenBooks
.com. Retrieved December 2013 (http://
johngreenbooks.com/paper-towns).

Green, John. "Will Grayson, Will Grayson."
JohnGreenBooks.com. Retrieved December
2013 (http://johngreenbooks.com/will
-grayson).

"Hospital Chaplain: The Miracle of Swindon
Town #33." YouTube video, 11:58, by han-
kgames, November 2, 2011. Accessed
December 2013.

"How to Become An Adult: Get an Ilene."
YouTube video, 3:38, by Vlogbrothers, August
31, 2011. Retrieved December 2013 (http://
www.youtube.com/watch?v=UBKKcxCuH-g).

Hubbard, Kim. "Live Chat with Author John
Green." *People*, August 22, 2013. Retrieved
December 2013 (http://www.people.com/
people/article/0,,20724883,00.html).

"I Am Not a Pornographer." YouTube video, 4:00,
by Vlogbrothers, January 30, 2008. Accessed

December 2013 (http://www.youtube.com/
watch?v=fHMPtYvZ8tM).

Johnson, Steve. "Author John Green Wins
Tribune's Young Adult Literary Prize." *Chicago
Tribune*, May 18, 2012. Retrieved December
2013 (http://articles.chicagotribune.com/2012-
05-18/entertainment/ct-ae-0520-john-green
-award-20120518_1_youtube-video-copernicus
-solar-system).

Kaufman, Leslie. "A Novelist and His Brother Sell
Out Carnegie Hall." *New York Times*, January
16, 2013. Retrieved January 2013 (http://www
.nytimes.com/2013/01/17/books/john-and
-hank-green-bring-their-show-to-carnegie
-hall.html?_r=2&adxnnl=1&adxnnlx=1391277770
-dfpaJhkOIKHIRhBdosqNOQ).

"Kenyon College Presents: Pensive Moments with
John Green." Video, 1:06. Retrieved January
2014 (http://johngreen.kenyon.edu).

"Life Is Weird. Also Beautiful." YouTube video,
3:09, by Vlogbrothers, February 21, 2012.
Retrieved December 2013 (http://www
.youtube.com/watch?v=SUVM6PgJjVI).

Maughan, Shannon. "An 'Awesome' Meetup."
Publisher's Weekly, January 6, 2013. Retrieved
December 2013 (http://www.publishersweekly
.com/pw/by-topic/childrens/childrens-industry

-news/article/55368-an-awesome-meetup.html).

McEvoy, Marc. "Interview: John Green." *Sydney Morning Herald*, January 21, 2012. Retrieved December 2013 (http://www.smh.com.au/ entertainment/books/interview-john-green -20120119-1q71w.html).

"Men Running on Tanks and the Truth About Book Editors." YouTube video, 3:48, by vlogbrothers, June 6, 2011. Retrieved December 2013 (http://www.youtube.com/ watch?v=oLwJT-HhhB0).

Minzesheimer, Bob. "John and Hank Green Rock Carnegie Hall." *USA Today*, January 16, 2013. Retrieved December 2013 (http://www .usatoday.com/story/life/books/2013/01/16 /john-green-hank-green-nerdfighters-fault -in-our-stars/1839151).

Nguyen, Vi-An. "Tribute to a Teen Muse from *The Fault in Our Stars* Author John Green." *Parade*, January 25, 2014. Retrieved January 2014 (http://parade.condenast.com/256468/ viannguyen/tribute-to-a-teen-muse-from -fault-in-our-stars-author-john-green).

"On Middle School Misery." YouTube video, 3:22, by vlogbrothers, November 19, 2013. Retrieved January 2014 (http://www.youtube.com/watch ?v=u90dGnKhhlk).

"Perspective." YouTube video, 3:30, by Vlogbrothers, October 29, 2013. Retrieved December 2013 (http://www.youtube.com/watch?v=5ooCeoh6608).

"See YA author John Green Hang Out with President Obama." *Los Angeles Times*, February 15, 2013. Retrieved December 2013 (http://articles.latimes.com/2013/feb/15/ entertainment/la-et-jc-see-author-john-green -hangout-with-president-obama-20130215).

"To: Kenyon College. Love, John Green." YouTube video, 2:55, by Vlogbrothers, December 4, 2012. Retrieved December 2013 (http://www.youtube.com/watch?v= x0s9B6QM-b0).

ABOUT THE AUTHOR

Christine Poolos is an editor and writer of books for young adults. She is a graduate of Colby College and New York University's Creative Writing Program. She lives in New York City.

PHOTO CREDITS

Cover, pp. 3, 7 Ben Gabbe/Getty Images; pp. 11, 45, 48, 66–67 Ton Koene/Gamma-Rapho/Getty Images; pp. 14, 38–39 © AP Images; p. 17 Ton Koene/age fotostock/SuperStock; pp. 18–19 Curt Smith/flickr.com/photos/curtsm/2957036064/CC-BY-2.0; pp. 22–23 © Sally Ryan/ZUMA Press; p. 28 Courtesy Everett Collection; p. 31 Tobias Hase/dpa/picture-alliance/Newscom; pp. 36–37, 59 Jerod Harris/WireImage/Getty Images; pp. 42–43, 80 Jeff Malet Photography/Newscom; p. 51 Tobias Hase/EPA/Landov; p. 54 © Beowulf Sheehan/ZUMA Press; p. 62 Gustavo Caballero/Getty Images; p. 64 David Livingston/Getty Images; pp. 70–71 © Joshua Sudock/The Orange County Register/ZUMA Press; pp. 74–75 Bloomberg/Getty Images; pp. 76–77 Alexander Tamargo/Getty Images; cover, interior pages (book) © www.istockphoto.com/Andrzej Tokarski; cover, interior pages (textured background) javarman/Shutterstock.com; interior pages (blue background) © iStockphoto.com/Sanpapol.

Designer: Nicole Russo; Editor: Tracey Baptiste; Photo Researcher: Karen Huang